WHAT'S SCIENCE?

The who, where, why and how!

Written by Frances Durkin

Illustrated by The Boy Fitz Hammond

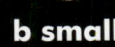

Published by b small publishing ltd. www.bsmall.co.uk © b small publishing ltd. 2023   1 2 3 4 5   ISBN 978-1-913918-68-2
Publisher: Sam Hutchinson   Art director: Vicky Barker   Designer: Karen Hood   Printed in Malta by Gutenberg Press
All rights reserved. No reproduction, copy or transmission of this publication may be made without written permission. No part of this publication may be reproduced, stored in a retrieval system or transmitted in any form or by any means, electronic, mechanical, photocopying, recording or otherwise, without the prior permission of the publisher. British Library Cataloguing in Publication Data. A catalogue record for this book is available from the British Library.

CONTENTS

4-5 A BURNING DISCOVERY
The incredible story of how humans learned to control fire

6-7 A WEIGHTY SUBJECT
How a falling apple inspired an extraordinary idea

8-9 THE CODE FOR LIFE
The secret information inside our cells

10-11 ATOMIC ENERGY
When the biggest power comes from the smallest thing

12-13 THE EXPLOSION AT THE START OF THE UNIVERSE
The theory about the beginning of everything

14-15 PROTECTION FROM ILLNESS
Did a cow really help to prevent a deadly disease?

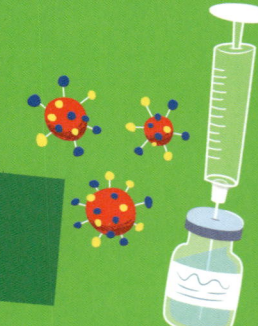

16-17 MINUTES, MONTHS, DAYS AND DATES
Why do we need to measure time?

18-19 MARVELLOUS MEDICINES
The surprising fighter in the battle against bad bacteria

20-21 SURVIVAL OF THE FITTEST
How evolution transforms entire species

22-23 THE TRANSFER OF ENERGY
The remarkable power of radiation

24-25 PAIN KILLER
The impact of anaesthesia

26-27 WHEN SPARKS FLY
Where does electricity come from?

28-29 WONDERFUL WAVES
A spectrum full of possibilities

30-31 GLOSSARY

32 TAKE IT FURTHER

A BURNING DISCOVERY

Fire was a crucial part of life for the earliest humans who used it for heat, light, cooking and for protection against predators. It became an important tool that changed the way people spent time together, as well as changing how they ate since cooking releases nutrients in some foods and makes them easier to digest. Archaeological evidence from a cave in modern-day Israel indicates that a fire in a **hearth** was used for cooking meat there 300,000 years ago.

flints

We don't know exactly when humans worked out how to start fire. Their first interactions with it were probably through lightning strikes and other accidental **ignitions**. Eventually flints were used to create sparks that started flames, which could be used in a controlled way.

300,000 years ago

Israel

Humans burned fires in hearths for cooking food, light and heating.

Recorded in the first century AD

Ancient Rome

Romans made matches from wooden sticks tipped with sulphur.

HOW TO MAKE FIRE

There are three things needed to make fire:

FIRE STARTERS

The control of fire continued to be important and new ways to start fires were invented. A lens could be used to focus sunlight on to a material that would burn and the heat would make it catch fire. Romans applied sulphur to the end of wooden sticks to make matches and this simple technology was recorded hundreds of years later in China and again in Europe in the nineteenth century. In 1826, a chemist called John Walker invented friction matches when he combined chemicals on the end of a stick and found that they caught fire when they were scraped.

1781 – 1859 AD

John Walker
Stockton-on-Tees, England

Walker invented a type of match that could be lit by scraping the chemical-coated end against a hard surface.

TAKE IT FURTHER

Preventing and putting out fires is an important part of controlling them. Firefighters existed in ancient Rome and ancient Egypt.

What can you find out about the history of fighting fires?

A WEIGHTY SUBJECT

When the seventeenth century mathematician Isaac Newton saw an apple fall from a tree, he realised that all objects in the universe were pulled together by an invisible **force**. He created a **mathematical equation** to show how the force pulling the two objects together is affected by their mass and the distance between them.

Before Newton's theory, the ancient Greeks thought that everything had its natural place in the universe and all objects would return to where they were meant to be. Newton was the first person to find a reason why things behaved in this way.

$$Fg = G \frac{m_1 m_2}{r^2}$$

1642 – 1727

Sir Isaac Newton
Grantham, England

After seeing an apple fall from a tree, Newton came up with a mathematical equation to explain the force that made it fall. That force was called 'gravity'.

1879 – 1955

Albert Einstein
Berlin, Germany

Einstein's theory of general relativity shows that gravity is caused by objects creating curves in **space-time**.

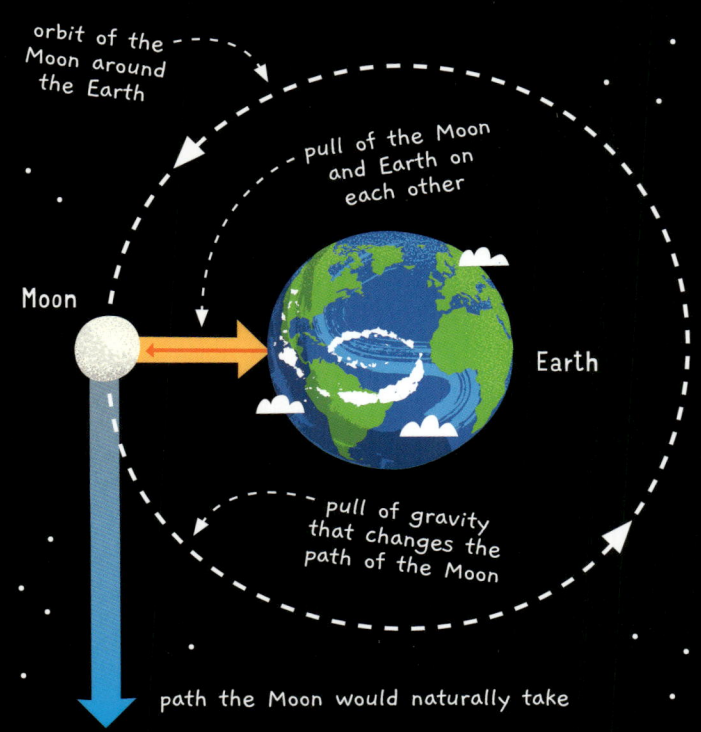

orbit of the Moon around the Earth
pull of the Moon and Earth on each other
Moon
Earth
pull of gravity that changes the path of the Moon
path the Moon would naturally take

Newton's equation showed that this force kept the Moon in orbit around Earth and the other planets circling around the Sun. He called the force 'gravity'.

WEIGHTLESS IN SPACE
Weight is the force of gravity on an object. Astronauts become weightless in the microgravity of space.

THE CURVE OF GENERAL RELATIVITY

In 1915, a physicist called Albert Einstein came up with the idea that objects bend the shape of space and time around them. He said that gravity is the result of **space-time** being curved towards an object.

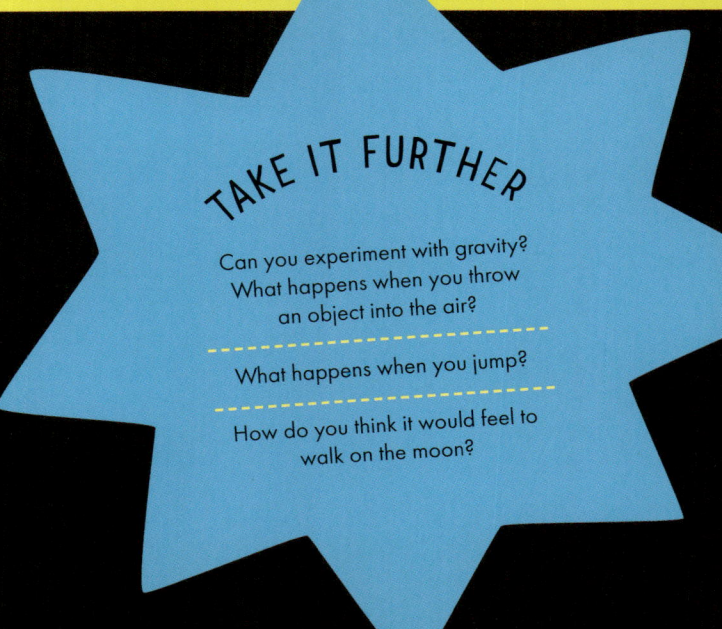

TAKE IT FURTHER

Can you experiment with gravity? What happens when you throw an object into the air?

What happens when you jump?

How do you think it would feel to walk on the moon?

THE CODE FOR LIFE

In 1869, a Swiss chemist named Friedrich Miescher tried to identify the parts of white blood cells by experimenting on pus from used bandages. He discovered a new molecule in the nucleus of the cells and he named it 'nuclein'. A few years later that substance was given the name DNA (deoxyribonucleic acid) and in the 1940s scientists found out that it contains the genetic information that living organisms pass from one generation to another.

A few years before Miescher's discovery, Gregor Mendel demonstrated that some characteristics of pea plants such as height, pod shape and colour were passed on to new generations by the dominant and recessive genes of each plant. This is called 'Mendelian inheritance' and it is caused by DNA.

Miescher experimented on pus from used bandages

WHAT IS DNA?

DNA contains the genetic information that all living things need to function and grow. It is made of two chains of chemicals called nucleotides that twist together to form a long spiral known as a double helix structure. There are four different types of nucleotides (adenine, cytosine, guanine and thymine) in DNA and, in different combinations, they make up the genetic code for all living things.

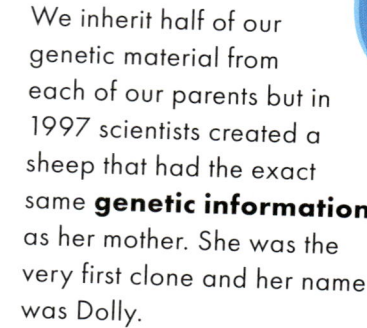

We inherit half of our genetic material from each of our parents but in 1997 scientists created a sheep that had the exact same **genetic information** as her mother. She was the very first clone and her name was Dolly.

A gene is a section of DNA that is responsible for a certain instruction or piece of information, such as eye colour and height.

1853 – 1927

Albrecht Kossel
Berlin, Germany

Kossel first used the name DNA and discovered that it was made up of the nitrogen bases adenine, cytosine, guanine and thymine.

1877 – 1955

Oswald Avery
New York, America

While researching bacterial pneumonia, Avery discovered that DNA carried genetic information.

1920 – 1958

Rosalind Franklin
London, England

Franklin took an X-ray diffraction photo of the helix form of DNA. This image was crucial to the research later published by James Watson and Francis Crick about the structure of DNA.

2003

The Human Genome Project sequenced the full chain of nucleotide pairs in the human body. It is more than 3 billion base pairs long.

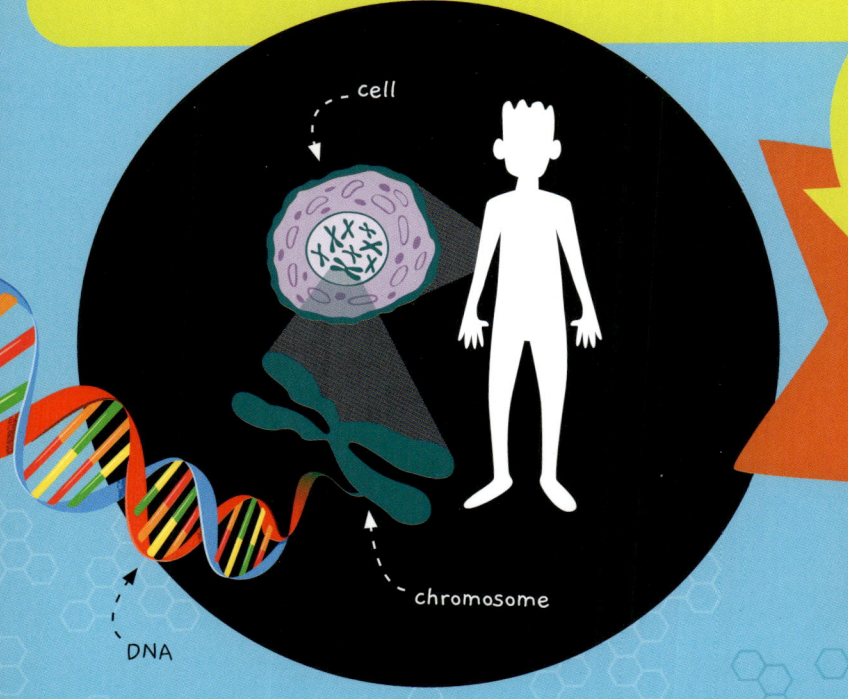

TAKE IT FURTHER

The Human Genome Project took more than 13 years to complete but it is now possible to have your personal genome sequenced in a day. It would show which genetic traits and diseases that you might be more likely to have.

Would you like to know what could happen to you later in your life, even if it might not happen?

ATOMIC ENERGY

In Italy in the 1930s, the physicist Enrico Fermi showed that bombarding a **stable element** with **neutrons** could change it and make it **radioactive**. Fermi believed he had created new elements. In 1938, an Austrian physicist named Lise Meitner explained what had really happened.

Meitner was one of a team of physicists who researched the effects of firing neutrons at an element called uranium. They discovered that an **atom** released a huge amount of energy when it was split into two smaller parts. The process was named nuclear fission.

Fission was very important and some scientists saw that if it were controlled and done slowly, the energy could be used to generate the power that people used in their homes.

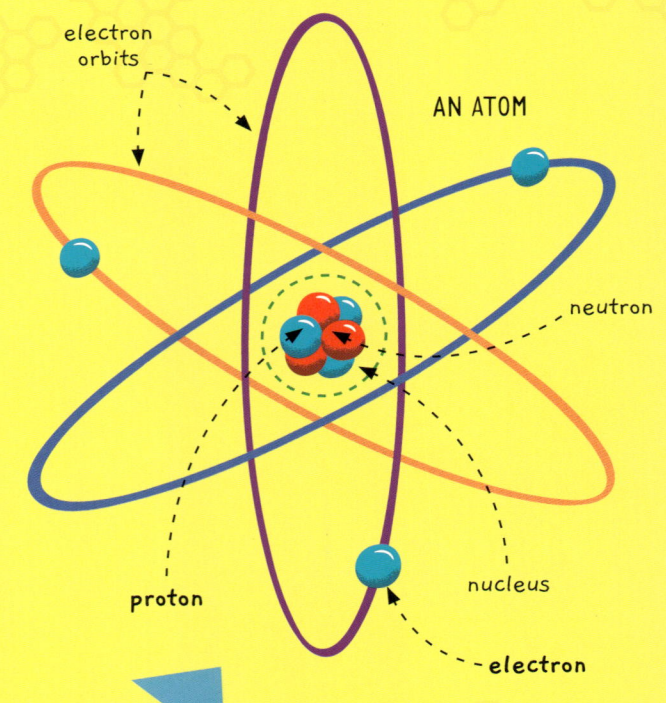

AN ATOM

electron orbits

neutron

proton

nucleus

electron

1901 - 1954

Enrico Fermi
Rome, Italy

Fermi fired subatomic particles called neutrons at atoms. This caused them to become radioactive.

1878 - 1968

Lise Meitner
Stockholm, Sweden

Meitner realised that the **nucleus** of an atom released a huge amount of energy when it was split into two smaller parts.

HOW FISSION POWERS POWER PLANTS

Nuclear fission is an efficient way to create the steam that power plants need to generate electricity. The core of a nuclear reactor is made from rods of uranium. When neutrons are fired at the rods, the atoms split, releasing energy and more neutrons. The neutrons hit and split other atoms, creating a chain reaction that makes the heat needed for steam.

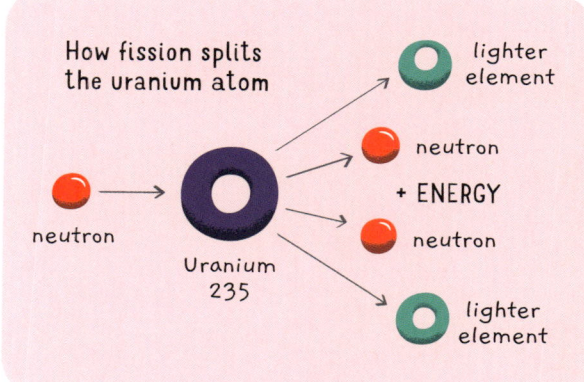

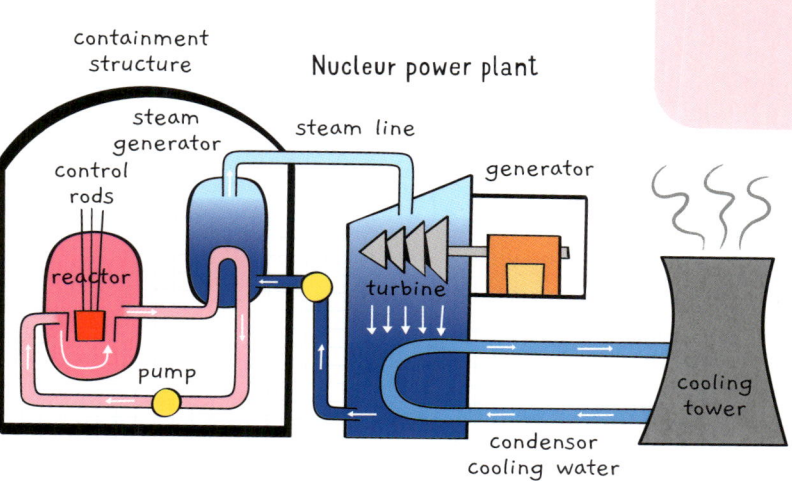

TAKE IT FURTHER

Is a scientist to blame for how their discovery is used?

Should they be responsible for making sure it is used in good ways?

Can they stop it from being used in ways that are harmful or dangerous?

THE DESTRUCTIVE POWER OF FISSION

During the Second World War, the American government invited Meitner to work on creating a nuclear weapon. She refused but some of her colleagues did join what was known as The Manhattan Project. In August 1945, their bombs were dropped on the Japanese cities of Nagasaki and Hiroshima.

FUN FACT Meitner's work on fission was largely unrecorded and she didn't get credit for her work. One of her colleagues was awarded the Nobel Prize in Chemistry but she was not. However, she was nominated for the Nobel Prize in Chemistry 19 times and the Nobel Prize in Physics 29 times.

THE EXPLOSION AT THE START OF THE UNIVERSE

In the 1920s, a theoretical physicist named Georges Lemaître observed that all the **galaxies** in the sky were moving further away from each other. He proposed that the universe was expanding but that everything in it must have started from the same place a very long time ago before moving apart. He called his idea the 'Cosmic Egg' and it later became known as the 'Big Bang'.

WHAT WAS THE BIG BANG?

The Big Bang theory proposes that a massive explosion created the universe 13.8 billion years ago. This sudden burst of energy was very dense and hot, but it grew and cooled. It created matter and atoms which formed into stars and galaxies.

Nobody knows why or how it happened.

1894 – 1966

Georges Lemaître
Louvain, Belgium

Lemaître proposed the 'Big Bang', which is considered the most likely explanation for the creation of the universe.

1933 & 1936

Arno Penzias (1933) **and Robert Wilson** (1936)
New Jersey, USA

Penzias and Wilson detected a strange sound when they were listening to radio waves from distant galaxies. They had discovered the remaining radiation energy from the Big Bang.

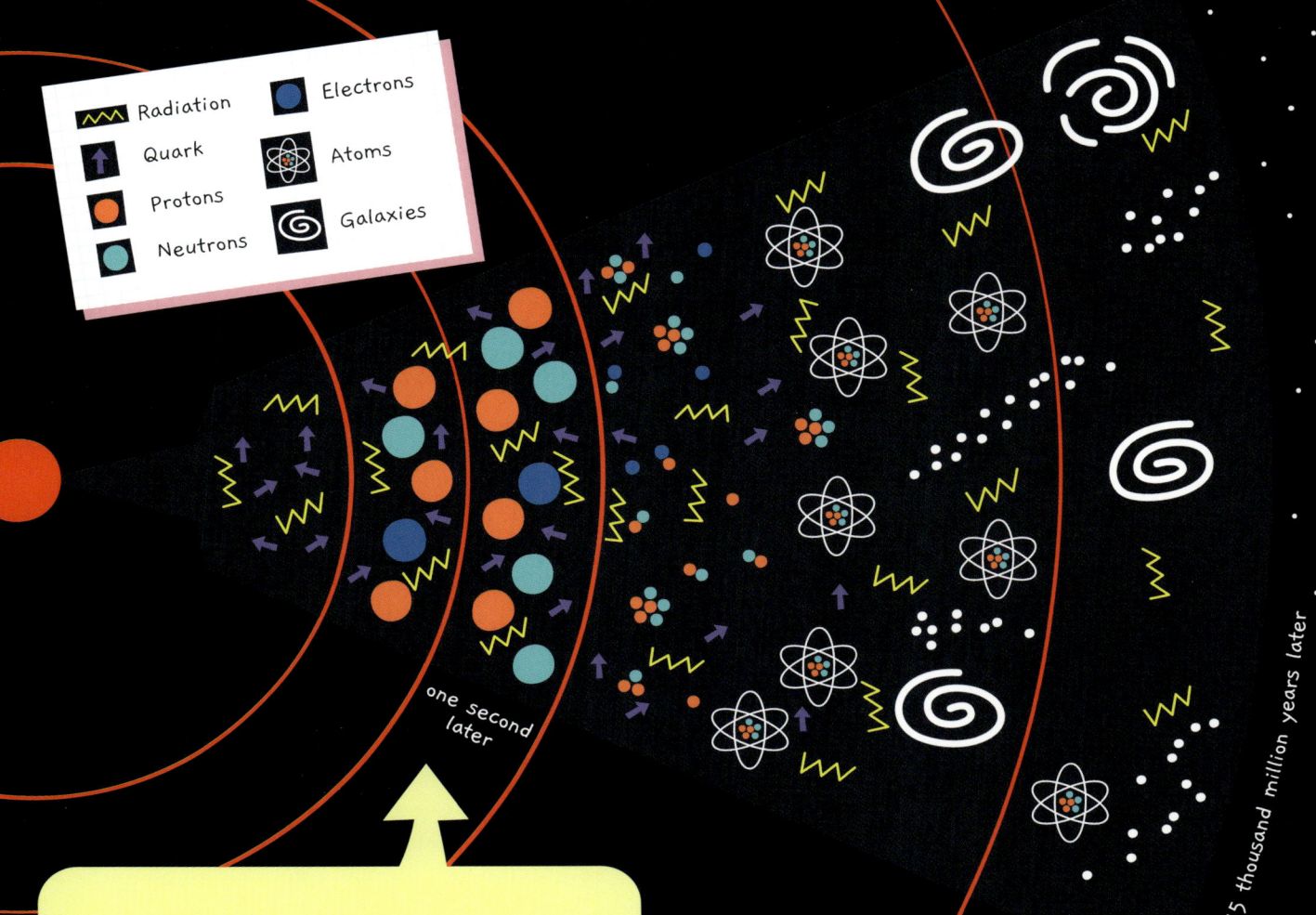

POSSIBLE PROOF OF THE THEORY

In 1965, two radio astronomers named Arno Penzias and Robert Wilson were using an **antenna** to measure **radio waves** from distant galaxies. They kept hearing a strange humming noise that they couldn't explain. At first, they thought it was because some pigeons had made a nest inside the antenna, so they got rid of the birds and cleaned up all the droppings. But the sound continued. Eventually they realised that the noise was a type of **radiation** called 'cosmic microwave background radiation'. It is the energy left over from the Big Bang and it exists all over the universe.

TAKE IT FURTHER

Today, scientists from all over the world are still investigating the Big Bang. Powerful telescopes can see further into space and observe how the universe is changing. Observe the night sky with a telescope, if you can find one.

Which stars or planets you can see?

PROTECTION FROM ILLNESS

In 1796, an English doctor called Edward Jenner realised that people who had caught a disease called cowpox seemed to be protected from a terrible illness called smallpox. He experimented with giving people cowpox to see if it would give them immunity against smallpox too. This was the first vaccine.

Before vaccination, variolation exposed people to smallpox by taking material from scabs or pustules and blowing it into their noses or scratching it into their arms. They would then catch the disease and develop immunity, but some people became so sick that they died. Jenner knew about this but he used material from a sore caused by cowpox because it was much safer and it still protected people from the more serious disease.

smallpox virus

c. 460 - 400 BC

Thucydides
Athens, Greece

In 430 BC Thucydides described how those who recovered from the plague were never affected by it again. This is thought to be one of the earliest written accounts of the effects of immunity.

1661 - 1722

Emperor K'ang Hsi
Beijing, China

Emperor K'ang Hsi had smallpox as a child. As an adult he ordered that variolation be used to protect his children from getting sick.

cowpox antibodies bind to and neutralise the smallpox virus

antigen

antigen-binding site

smallpox virus

antibody

WHAT IS A VACCINE?
Vaccines give us the tools we need to fight against illnesses. When our bodies are exposed to antigens (these are anything that trigger an immune response, such as bacteria or a virus) our immune system makes special proteins called antibodies that lock on to them and fight off the illness. After we have recovered, those antibodies are stored as memory cells and they provide immunity against that specific antigen in the future. Vaccines force our immune system to make the right antibodies to protect us.

Cowpox gave us the word 'vaccine' because vacca is the Latin word for 'cow'.

WHAT IS THE HERD EFFECT?
A disease cannot spread easily to people who are immune. When a large number of people have immunity, the disease can slow or stop completely. This helps to protect people who don't or can't have the vaccine. Lots of diseases have been wiped out or are now kept under control by vaccines. This has saved thousands of people's lives from terrible illnesses including polio, flu, diphtheria, measles, mumps, malaria, COVID-19 and many more.

TAKE IT FURTHER
Vaccinations can save many people's lives, but do you think that everyone should have them?

How should we protect people who cannot have vaccinations?

1749 - 1823

1980

Edward Jenner
Berkley, England

Edward Jenner, a country doctor, made a vaccine for smallpox from the disease cowpox.

The World Health Organisation **(WHO)** declared the world to be free of smallpox

15

MINUTES, MONTHS, DAYS AND DATES

The ancient Romans used a ten-month calendar that began in the spring and lasted for around 304 days. Two more months were created in 713 BC but the year added up to 355 days. The calendar didn't match up with the seasons and people became very confused. Finally, in the first century AD, Roman emperor Julius Caesar borrowed from the Greek and Egyptian calendars to make a year that was 365 days long but had one extra day every four years.

It became known as the Julian calendar and was used across much of Europe.

THE GREGORIAN CALENDAR

In the 1500s, people realised that spring was starting earlier in the year. This was because a year is actually 365.2425 days long. That's about 11 minutes shorter than in the Julian calendar. Pope Gregory XIII removed ten days from October in 1582 and from years ending in '00' unless it was possible to divide that year by 400. The pope only had the power to impose his new calendar in the places that were ruled by the Catholic church. It took a very long time for it to become the most common calendar around the world and Greece didn't adopt it until 1923. Today some countries use the Gregorian calendar alongside their own calendars and others do not use it at all.

100 BC – 44 BC

Julius Caesar
Rome, Italy

Julius Caesar changed the Roman calendar to last a full 365 days and added a leap year every four years.

1502 – 1585

Pope Gregory XIII
Rome, Italy

The pope authorised a change to the Julian calendar that brought it back into line with the seasons and catholic festivals.

TAKE IT FURTHER

The ancient Romans named the months after gods, festivals and numbers. December comes from the Latin word for 'ten' because it was their tenth month and March was named in honour of the god Mars. July gets its name from Emperor Julius Caesar.

Can you think of new names for the months?

FUN FACTS
- Calendars have always been important to the celebration of religious festivals.
- Afghanistan, Ethiopia, Iran and Nepal do not use the Gregorian Calendar.
- The Aztec calendar had 18 months.

MARVELLOUS MEDICINES

In 1928, a scientist called Alexander Fleming was researching a type of bacteria called staphylococcus. He went away without cleaning up and returned two weeks later to find a strange mould developing on one of his Petri dishes. He realised that this mould had stopped the bacteria from growing. He named his discovery 'penicillin' and it became a very important medicine that could be used to treat all kinds of bacterial infections, including pneumonia and tonsillitis.

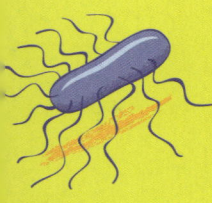

The idea that bacteria can cause illnesses was proposed by a French biologist named Louis Pasteur in the 1860s. He was investigating disease in silkworms and proved that bacterial **microbes** were causing the sickness. His idea came to be known as 'germ theory'.

1822 – 1895
Louis Pasteur
Strasbourg, France

Pasteur realised that tiny microbes including bacteria could cause diseases.

1827 – 1912
Joseph Lister
Glasgow, Scotland

Lister protected his patients from infection by using antiseptic.

The study of germ theory inspired a surgeon called Joseph Lister to apply the ideas to his work. He was the first person to use **antiseptics** to clean his surgical equipment and he was careful to protect his patients from infection.

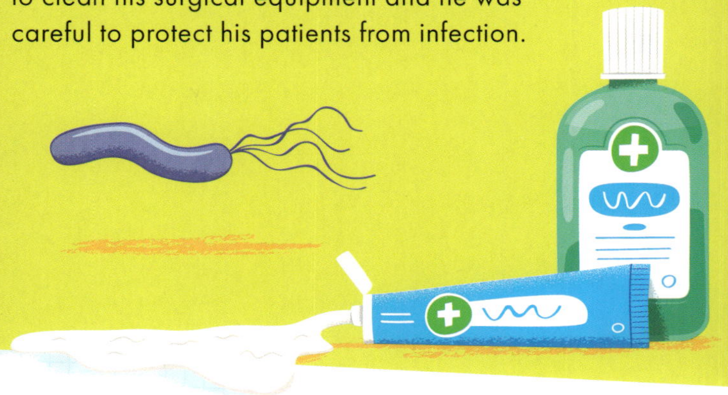

ANTIBIOTIC RESISTANCE

In 1945, Fleming warned that bacteria were able to **evolve** and that they could become resistant to antibiotics. He was right and, although many new antibiotics have been developed since the 1920s, some bacteria are unaffected by them. Bacteria that are resistant to more than one kind of antibiotic are called 'superbugs'.

WHAT IS BACTERIA?

Bacteria are tiny, single-celled organisms that live everywhere. Most of them are completely harmless but some do cause illnesses and infections.

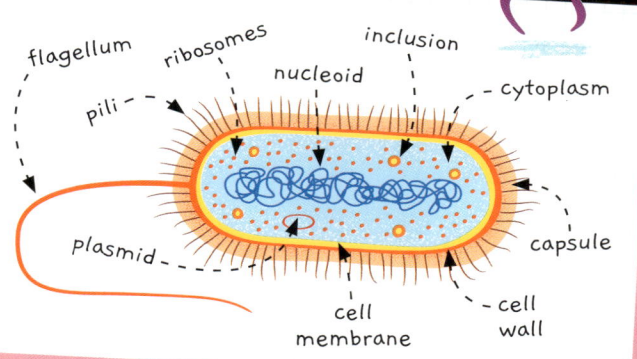

1881 – 1955

Alexander Fleming
London, England

Fleming accidentally exposed the bacteria he was studying to mould spores, which stopped it from growing. He had discovered the first antibiotic.

TAKE IT FURTHER

How do you prevent the spread of germs in your home?

Do you wash your hands?

Do you cover your mouth when you sneeze?

SURVIVAL OF THE FITTEST

In 1831, a naturalist called Charles Darwin was part of an expedition to explore South America. His ship stopped at the Galapagos Islands where he observed the different species of animals on each of the islands. Darwin noticed that some of the birds had different shaped heads and beaks. They were all related to the same **ancestor**, but they had adapted to eat different kinds of foods. He called this 'natural selection'.

Darwin was not the first person to see that species change according to their environments. The Chinese philosopher Zhuang Zhou had observed this in the fourth century BC and a man called Alfred Russell Wallace came up with the idea at the same time as Darwin.

Geospiza magnirostris

Geospiza fortis

Geospiza parvula

Certhidea olivacea

WHAT IS NATURAL SELECTION?

Natural selection is when the genetic characteristics of a species change to suit their environment over time. A species may adapt to changes, such as new predators or new diseases. If an individual has a feature that gives it an advantage, it is more likely to survive and pass its beneficial genes on to the next generation.

We are Darwin's finches. Can you see our different shaped beaks for crushing or digging up our food?

c. 369 BC – 289 BC

Zhuang Zhou
China

Zhuang was a philosopher who realised that all animals have characteristics that suit the environments where they live.

1809 – 1882

Charles Darwin
Downe, England

Darwin came up with the theory of natural selection.

HUMAN EVOLUTION

Human evolution is the idea that humans developed from the same common ancestor as apes. This process took millions of years, but we are all part of the **primate** family. We share lots of characteristics with other primates including **opposable thumbs** and forward-facing eyes. Archaeological research and DNA technology have discovered that many different early humans lived at the same time as our species, *Homo sapiens*.

Humans share 99.8% of our DNA with chimpanzees.

TAKE IT FURTHER

Can you think of other animals that have adapted to suit their environment?

Why do you think that giraffes have long necks?

Why do some primates have tails?

21

THE TRANSFER OF ENERGY

In 1896, a physicist named Henri Becquerel accidentally discovered radiation after leaving some uranium on a photographic plate. Some elements, such as uranium, are unstable and release particles of energy until they become stable again. The photographic plate registered these particles! Becquerel's student, Marie Curie, called this process **radioactive decay** or radioactivity.

There are three main types of radioactive decay, each releasing particles of energy in different ways:

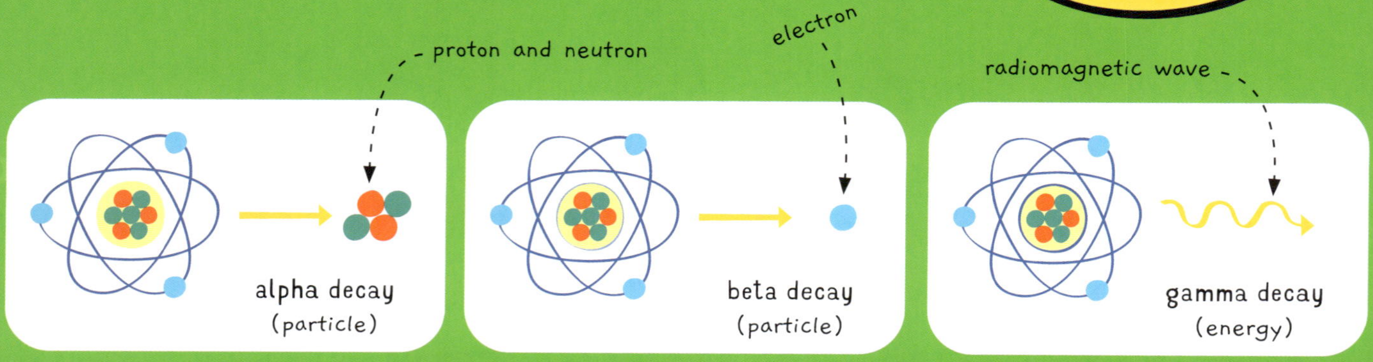

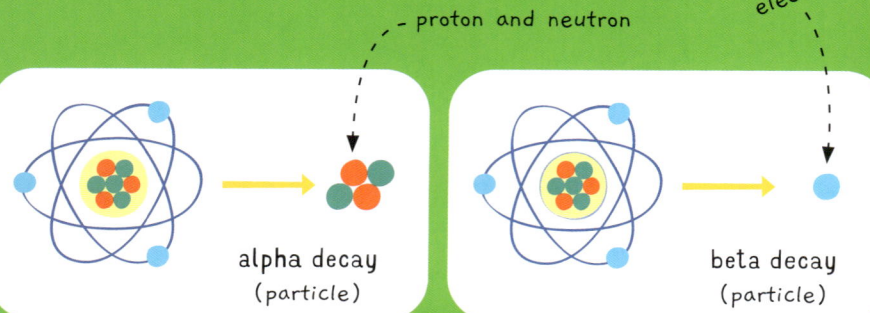

alpha decay (particle) — proton and neutron
beta decay (particle) — electron
gamma decay (energy) — radiomagnetic wave

Henri Becquerel
Paris, France
1852 – 1908

Becquerel accidentally discovered radioactivity when he left uranium on a photographic plate in a drawer.

Marie Curie
Paris, France
1867 – 1934

Curie came up with the word 'radioactivity' and discovered two radioactive elements. She is the only person to have won Nobel prizes for both Chemistry and Physics.

THE POWER OF RADIOACTIVITY

Marie Curie and her husband, Pierre, discovered two new radioactive chemical elements that they named polonium and radium. During the First World War, Marie Curie created a portable X-ray machine, using radium, that could be installed in a vehicle and driven to wherever it was needed for injured soldiers. She raised the money for the vehicles, developed a generator that could power the X-ray, trained women to operate them and even drove one herself. They were nicknamed 'little Curies'.

RADIATION MEDICINE

Wilhelm Röntgen used gamma rays from radium to create a medical treatment called 'radiation therapy'. This was successfully used to treat cancer but too much exposure to this **ionising radiation** can cause damage to living cells. Marie Curie became very sick and died after spending so much of her career working with these materials.

My possessions will be radioactive for the next 1,500 years!

TAKE IT FURTHER

Marie Curie was a scientist who worked in a world that was dominated by men. Why do you think that women are underrepresented in the history of science?

Can you find out about a historical female scientist, from anywhere in the world, who made an amazing discovery?

PAIN KILLER

In 1846, American dentist William Morton used a gas called ether to stop a patient from feeling pain during an operation. His method of giving pain relief meant that patients could have safe and painless medical procedures. Medicines that numb pain or send a patient to sleep during an operation are called anaesthetics.

You won't feel a thing!

Morton was not the first person to experiment with pain relief and he had experience of using a gas called nitrous oxide in his dental work. This substance was also known as 'laughing gas' but it didn't always work so Morton set out to find something better.

Before anaesthetic, surgery was a traumatic and agonising experience. Many patients died from shock so physicians and scientists spent centuries searching for a way to ease their pain. The earliest records show that they used plants and herbs. Historical books from China record a doctor named Hua Tou using a herbal anaesthetic called 'mafeisan' in the second century AD. **Chloroform** was commonly used during the nineteenth century.

---

c. 140 – 208 AD

Hua Tou
China

Hua Tou was a Chinese physician who is said to have used a herbal mixture as a painkiller.

1819 – 1868

William Morton
Boston, Massachusetts, USA

Morton was a dentist who successfully used a gas called 'ether' to stop a patient from feeling pain during an operation.

HOW DOES ANAESTHESIA WORK?

The human body is an incredible thing that uses neurones to send messages to the brain. If we have toothache or a stubbed toe, our brain receives a message to tell us that we are in pain. Anaesthesia stops the nerves from sending pain messages.

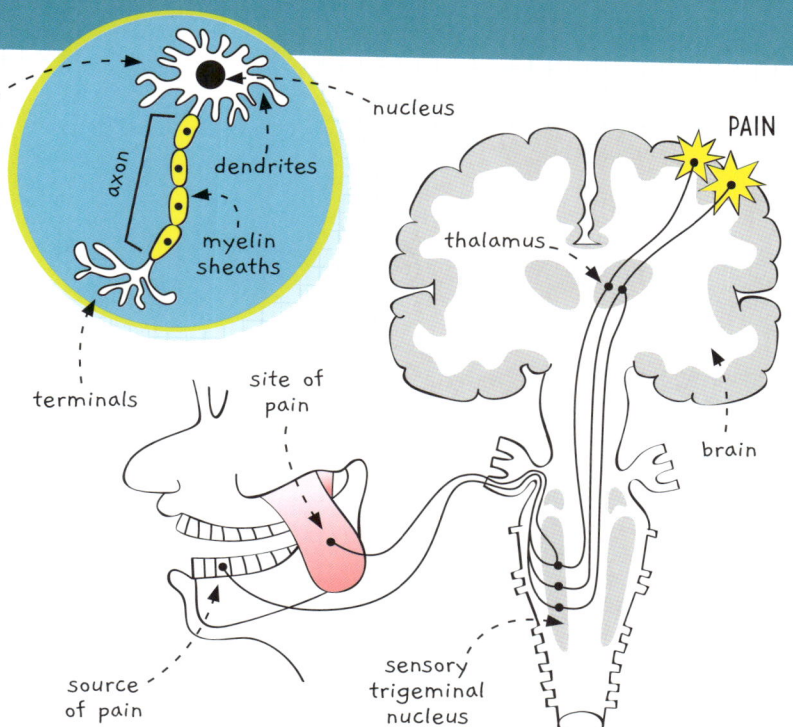

Modern anaesthesia is much safer than ether and chloroform. It can even be used to numb the pain in very specific areas. This is called 'local anaesthetic' and was invented by eye surgeon Karl Koller in 1884 when he put the painkiller directly on to his patient's eyeball.

1857 – 1944

Karl Koller
Vienna, Austria

Koller invented local anaesthetic by putting the painkiller directly on to the area he needed to operate on.

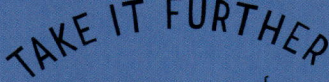

TAKE IT FURTHER

Before the invention of anaesthetic, surgery was very dangerous and difficult. How do you think it changed afterwards?

And do you think that it allowed for new procedures to take place that were not possible before?

25

WHEN SPARKS FLY

The Greek philosopher Thales of Miletus noticed that if amber were rubbed with fur or silk, very light objects such as straw and feathers would stick to it. This attraction was caused by **static electricity**. In 1600, an English scientist called William Gilbert described this **phenomenon** as 'electricus' from the Greek word for amber, which later became 'electricity'.

In 1752, the American scientist Benjamin Franklin famously proved that lightning was a form of electricity by flying a kite with a key attached to it when a thunderstorm was approaching. The key picked up the electric charge from the storm and Franklin felt a spark when he touched it.

What an electrifying experiment!

c. 623 – 545 BC

Thales of Miletus
Miletus, Ancient Greece (present-day Turkey)

Thales observed static electric charge when a piece of amber was rubbed with fabric. It attracted small objects that became attached to it.

1544 – 1603

William Gilbert
London, England

Gilbert studied the difference between magnetism and static electricity. He came up with the name 'electricus'.

AC OR DC?

In the late 1870s, the American inventor Thomas Edison created a system for supplying electricity to houses, shops and factories. He used 'direct current' (DC) which was a continuous flow of electricity in the same direction along a wire. But DC was difficult to convert to different **voltages** and it could only travel for short distances. His rival, George Westinghouse, worked with Nikola Tesla to create a supply which ran on the 'alternating current' (AC). AC flows backwards and forwards, can change to different voltages and can travel over greater distances. Their battle to become the primary supplier of electricity in North America was known as the 'War of the Currents' and today most electricity runs on alternating current. Batteries produce direct current.

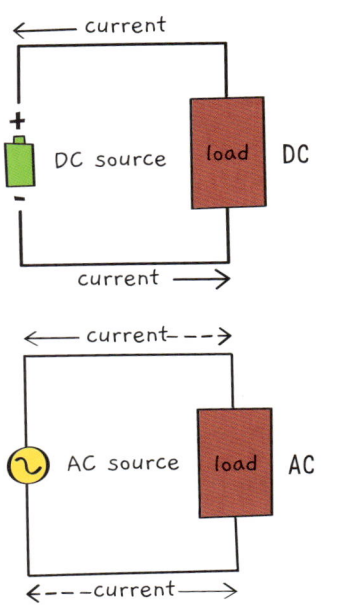

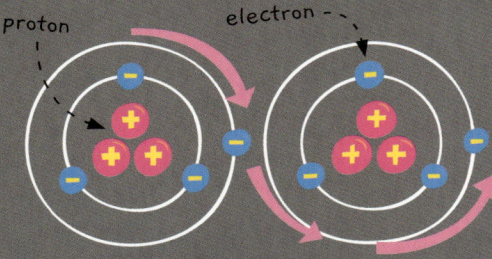

The flow of electrons between atoms

WHAT IS ELECTRICITY?

Electricity is a type of energy. It is caused by the flow or presence of charged **particles** in an atom. An atom is made of particles called protons, electrons, and neutrons. Protons carry a positive electrical charge and electrons carry a negative electrical charge. The flow of electrons between atoms creates electricity.

1856 – 1943

Nikola Tesla
New York, USA

Worked with George Westinghouse to supply electricity to as many people as possible by using 'alternating current'.

TAKE IT FURTHER

Electricity is generated in lots of different ways. Can you think of natural ways to create energy?

Why do you think it is important to use renewable energy sources?

27

WONDERFUL WAVES

In 1895, a German physicist called Wilhelm Röntgen discovered a new type of invisible radiation. It contained so much energy that it could pass through skin and fat, but it was partially blocked by muscle, and it was completely blocked by bone. He named this radiation X-rays and he used it to take a picture of the skeleton inside the hand of his wife, Anna Bertha Ludwig. She was very alarmed to see the bones under her skin but this new discovery allowed doctors to help their patients by looking inside them.

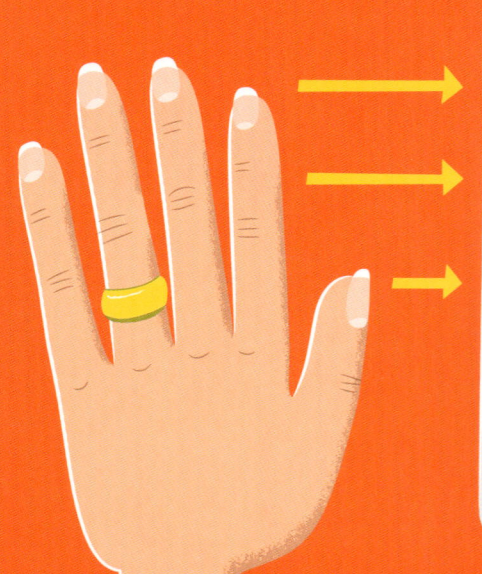
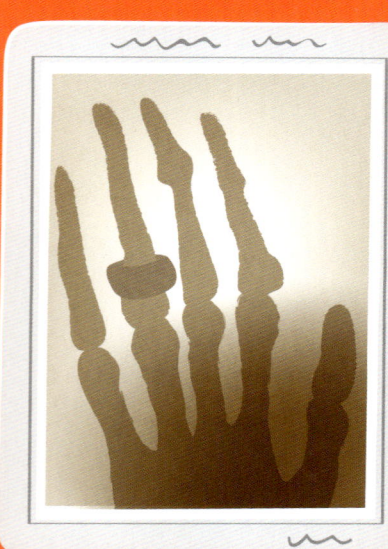

1831 – 1879

James Clerk Maxwell
London, England

Maxwell proposed that waves of electric and magnetic energy travel together at the speed of light.

1845 – 1923

Wilhelm Röntgen
Würzburg, Germany

Röntgen discovered a high energy radiation that could pass through more materials than other types of electromagnetic wave. He had discovered X-rays.

Röntgen knew that forms of energy were all around, even if he could not see them. Thirty years before, in 1865, the Scottish scientist James Clerk Maxwell had suggested that electric and magnetic radiation travelled together in waves of energy. He said that light was a visible form of this energy and he predicted other invisible waves too, such as Röntgen's X-rays.

WHAT ARE ELECTROMAGNETIC WAVES?

When electric fields and magnetic fields travel together they carry packets of energy called **photons** in movements called waves. The distance between each of these waves as they move up and down is called a wavelength, or **frequency**. Waves that are long have a low frequency and carry less energy. X-rays are short waves that have a high frequency and carry more energy.

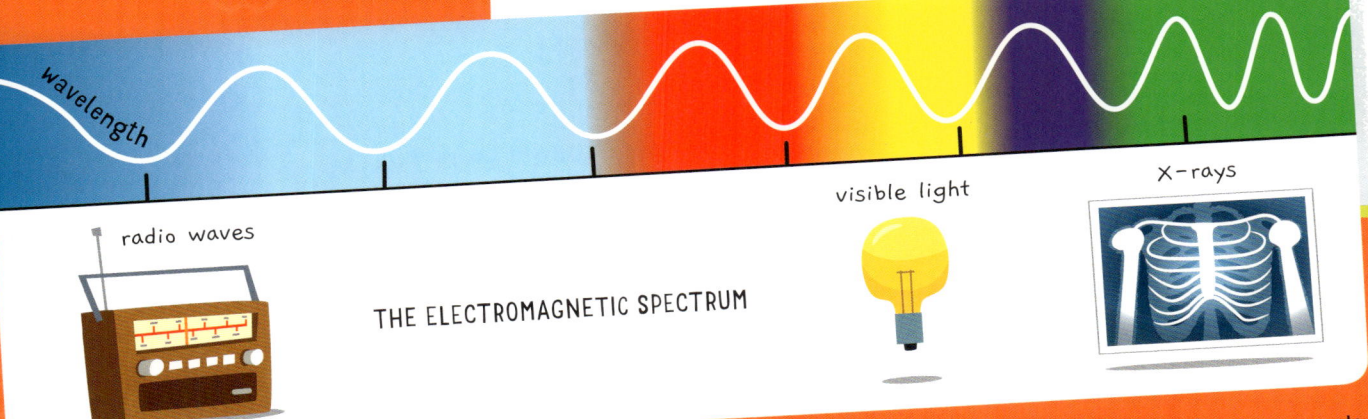

THE ELECTROMAGNETIC SPECTRUM

X-rays are a type of **ionising radiation** which can be harmful in large amounts.

TAKE IT FURTHER

Make a shadow show.
Shadows are created by blocking the energy from a light source. If you hold your hand in front of a light it will cast a shadow that is the same shape as your hand. But what happens to the shadow if you hold a piece of fabric or tissue paper in front of the light instead? Does some of the light energy still travel through? What if you use coloured tissue? Can you make a shadow puppet out of cardboard and tissue?

FUN FACTS

Röntgen won the first ever Nobel Prize for Physics in 1901 for his discovery of X-rays. He never took out patents on his discovery because he thought it should be free for everyone.

GLOSSARY

Ancestor
a person in your family who lived a long time ago.

Antenna
a device that sends or receives radio waves.

Antiseptic
a substance that reduces the growth of microorganisms.

Atom
a very small building block for all the matter in the universe.

Chloroform
a liquid that was once used as an anaesthetic.

Electron
a negatively charged sub-atomic particle.

Evolve
when something, often a species, changes or develops gradually over a long period of time.

Force
a power that can change how an object moves.

Frequency
how quickly a wave of energy moves up and down.

Galaxy
a group of stars with clouds of gas, dust and dark matter.

Genetic information
the biological instructions that pass down from generation to generation.

Hearth
the floor of a fireplace.

Ignition
the action that starts a fire.

Ionising radiation
a form of energy that can remove an electron from a molecule or atom.

Mathematical equation
a mathematical way of writing that two things are equal to each other, for example $2+2=4$.

Microbes
tiny organisms that can only be seen through a microscope.

Neurone
a nerve cell that sends information throughout the body.

Neutron
a subatomic particle found in the nucleus of almost all atoms.

Nucleus (atom)
the central part of an atom made up of protons and neutrons.

Nucleus (cell)
the structure within a cell that contains genetic information.

Opposable thumb
can be placed against a finger in order to pick something up.

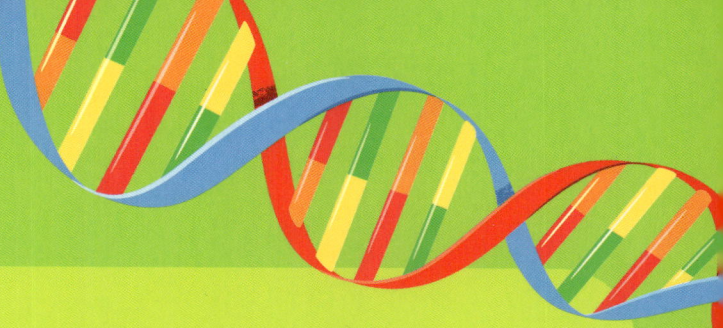

Particles
very small pieces of something.

Phenomenon
a thing or event that can be observed.

Photon
a tiny particle of light or electromagnetic radiation.

Primate
a member of an order of mammals that includes humans, monkeys and apes.

Proton
a subatomic particle with a positive electrical charge.

Radiation
the sending of energy in the form of waves or particles during radioactive decay.

Radio wave
a type of electromagnetic radiation with the longest wavelength.

Radioactive decay
when the nucleus of an unstable atom loses energy and gives off radiation.

Radioactivity
when something produces energy in the form of radiation.

Space-time
a mathematical model that combines space and time to show how the universe works.

Stable element
a chemical element that does not decay over time.

Static electricity
when an object has a build-up of an electric charge on its surface that doesn't move.

Tissue
a group of cells that have similar structures and functions.

Voltage
the pressure from an electrical power source that makes electrically charged particles move.

WHO
the World Health Organisation is responsible for promoting good health all over the world.

TAKE IT FURTHER

The extraordinary scientists that we have met in this book made their discoveries by questioning the world around them. They wanted to know how things worked and why, so they used the scientific method:

- observation
- research
- testing a hypothesis (theory)
- analysing the data
- reaching a conclusion

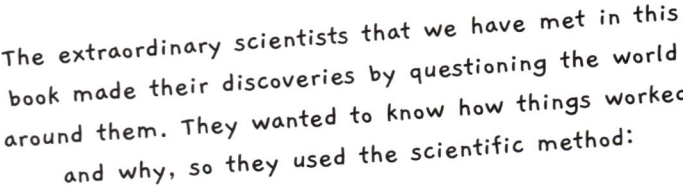

Their work has uncovered incredible knowledge that they have shared so that we can also understand the world. The Latin word 'scientia' actually means knowledge. Which scientific discovery was your favourite?

There are still so many unanswered questions about the world that scientists will never run out of ideas to test and knowledge to share.

Can you think of any scientific questions that you'd like to answer? Maybe you'd like to know more about different kinds of weather. Or what about the number of species of spider in your house? Your question could be simple or complex, but it could be the beginning of some amazing research that leads to some brand-new knowledge.

The future of science is limitless!